PYTHONFLOW: MASTERING MACHINE LEARNING FROM BASICS TO BRILLIANCE

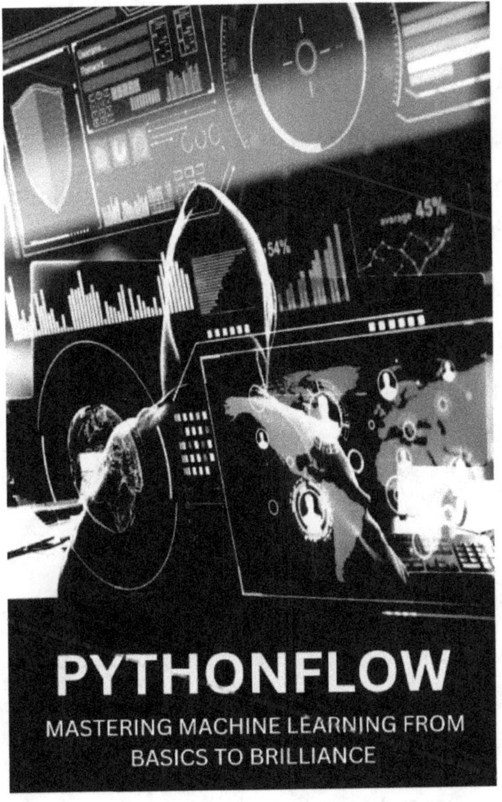

Contents

4

Section 1: Prologue to AI

1.1 What is AI?

AI is a field of man-made reasoning (simulated intelligence) that spotlights on the improvement of calculations and models that empower PCs to gain from information and pursue forecasts or choices without being expressly modified. Basically, about making frameworks can consequently gain and improve for a fact.

1.2 Types of Machine Learning

Machine learning can be broken down into a number of different types, each of which serves a distinct purpose:

1.2.1 Regulated Learning

In regulated learning, the calculation is prepared on a marked dataset, where each information has a relating yield. The objective is to gain a planning from contributions to yields, making it equipped for making expectations on new, concealed information.

1.2.2 Solo Learning

Solo learning manages unlabeled information, meaning to track down examples, connections, or designs inside the information. Normal undertakings incorporate bunching comparable data of interest or decreasing the dimensionality of the information.

1.2.3 Support Learning

Support learning includes a specialist that figures out how to settle on choices by cooperating with a climate. The specialist gets criticism as remunerations or punishments, permitting it to become familiar with the ideal conduct through experimentation.

1.3 Machine Learning's Applications

Machine learning can be used in a lot of different fields. A few normal applications include:

Picture and Discourse Acknowledgment: Perceiving objects in pictures or translating verbally expressed words.

Systems for Recommendation: Suggesting items or content in view of client inclinations.

Prescient Examination: Anticipating future patterns or ways of behaving in light of verifiable information.

Normal Language Handling (NLP): Understanding and producing human language.

1.4 Python and AI

Python has turned into the true language for AI because of its effortlessness, intelligibility, and a rich environment of libraries. A few well known libraries for AI in Python include:

NumPy: for manipulating arrays and doing numerical operations.
Pandas: For information control and examination.
Matplotlib and Seaborn: For information representation.
Scikit-Learn: An AI library with devices for order, relapse, grouping, and that's just the beginning.
Understanding the rudiments of Python and these libraries is fundamental for getting everything rolling with AI.

This section gives a fundamental comprehension of what AI is, its sorts, applications, and the job of Python in carrying out AI arrangements. Ensuing sections will dive further into each sort of AI and pragmatic executions.

Part 2: Setting Up Your Man-made awareness Environment

2.1 Introducing Python and the Boa

Constrictor to begin your electronic thinking association, you ought to at first set up your headway environment. Follow these pushes toward present the Boa constrictor and Python:

2.1.1 A Structure of Python

Download the latest variety of Python from python.org.

During establishment, attempt to truly look at the choice to add Python to your framework's Way.

2.1.2 Introducing Boa constrictor

Download and introduce Boa constrictor from the power site.

Python and a number of pre-installed libraries for data science and machine learning are included with Anaconda.

2.2 Introduction to Jupyter Scratch pad

Jupyter Scratch pad give a common habitat to making and running code, making them ideal for information assessment and assessment. To get everything moving, follow these methods:

2.2.1 Making Jupyter Scratch cushion Organized Open a terminal or the sales brief.

Type jupyter journal and press Enter.

Another tab will open in your web program with the Jupyter dashboard.

2.2.2 Making Your Most Famous Scratch Cushion To make a subsequent Python scratch cushion,

select "Python 3" from the "New" menu.

Code cells can be made and executed one by one, simplifying it to test and imagine results.

Section 3: Exploratory Information Investigation (EDA)

3.1 Stacking and Reviewing Information

Prior to jumping into AI, it's fundamental to comprehend and really get to know the dataset. This includes stacking the information into your current circumstance and examining its design. Follow this procedure:

3.1.1 Stacking Information with Pandas

python
Duplicate code

```python
import pandas as pd


# Load information from a CSV record
information = pd.read_csv('your_dataset.csv')
```

Show the initial not many columns of the dataset

```
print(data.head())
```

3.1.2 Reviewing Information

Check the aspects utilizing data.shape.

Investigate information types with data.dtypes.

Use data.info() to get an outline of the dataset.

3.2 Data Cleaning

The data must be cleaned in order for EDA to be accurate and meaningful. Normal undertakings incorporate taking care of missing qualities, eliminating copies, and tending to anomalies:

3.2.1 Dealing with Missing Qualities

python

Duplicate code

```
# Check for missing qualities
print(data.isnull().sum())
```

```python
# Drop columns with missing qualities
data_cleaned = data.dropna()
```

```python
# Fill missing qualities with a particular worth
data_filled = data.fillna(value)
```

3.2.2 Eliminating Copies

python

Duplicate code

```python
# Check for copy columns
print(data.duplicated().sum())
```

```python
# Eliminate copies
data_no_duplicates = data.drop_duplicates()
```

3.3 Clear Insights

Clear insights give an outline of the principal parts of the dataset:

3.3.1 Summary Statistics Python

Copy Code # Display summary

statistics print(data.describe())
3.3.2 Correlation Analysis Python Copy Code # Calculate correlation matrix correlation_matrix = data.corr() # Visualize correlation matrix import seaborn as sns sns.heatmap(correlation_matrix, annot=True, cmap='coolwarm')

3.4.1 Histograms

python
Duplicate code

```python
# Plot a histogram
import matplotlib.pyplot as plt
data['feature'].hist(bins=20)
plt.xlabel('Feature')
plt.ylabel('Frequency')
plt.title('Histogram of an Element')
plt.show()
```

3.4.2 Disperse Plots
python
Duplicate code

```python
# Make a disperse plot
```

```python
plt.scatter(data['feature1'], data['feature2'])
plt.xlabel('Feature 1')
plt.ylabel('Feature 2')
plt.title('Scatter Plot between Element 1 and Component 2')
plt.show()
```

This section outfits you with the abilities to load, clean, and investigate your dataset, establishing the groundwork for informed dynamic in later phases of the AI cycle. Ensuing parts will dig into building and assessing AI models in light of your EDA experiences.

Fourth Portion: 4.1 An Overview of Controlled Learning

Directed learning involves building a model from a checked dataset, with the computation deciding how to design input features in relation to studying yield names. As it explains the fundamentals of regulated learning, this section emphasizes the distinction between names and features.

4.2 Direct Apostatize

Direct lose the confidence is an enormous evaluation for predicting a reliable outcome. It shows the connection between free factors and a dependent variable, anticipating a straight relationship.

4.2.1 Directly Losing Faith in Python Duplicate code from sklearn.linear_model import

LinearRegression from sklearn.model_selection import train_test_split from sklearn.metrics import mean_squared_error # Divide the data into highlights and names X = data[['feature1', 'feature2']] y = data['target'] # Divide the data into arranging and testing sets X_ mse}')

4.3 Key Apostatize

Key apostatize is used for identical game plan issues, where the goal is to expect one of two probably results.

4.3.1 Utilizing Key Break faith

Python Duplicate code from sklearn.linear_model import LogisticRegression from sklearn.metrics import accuracy_score, classification_report # Expecting "target" is twofold (0 or 1) # In the

event that it has more classes, think about utilizing multinomial decided apostatize # Cause a fundamental to lose the faith model logistic_model = LogisticRegression() # Train the model logistic_model.fit(X_train, y_train) # Make gauges on the accuracy}')
print(f'Classification Report:\n{report}')

4.4 Decision Trees

Decision trees are adaptable models used for both collecting and fall away from the confidence endeavors. Because of their dynamic in light of part esteems, a tree-like plan arises.

4.4.1 Executing Choice Trees in Python Copy the code from sklearn.tree and import DecisionTreeClassifier and DecisionTreeRegressor. # For grouping, use tree_classifier = DecisionTreeClassifier() predictions_tree_classifier = tree_classifier.predict(X_test) # For relapse, use tree_re = DecisionTreeRegressor() tree_

4.5.1 Utilizing Random Forests

Copy the code from sklearn

4.6.1 Social event assessments in Python

Duplicate code from sklearn.metrics import accuracy_score, precision_score, recall_score, and f1_score # It is possible to Anticipate gauges exactness = accuracy_score(y_test, presumptions) precision = precision_score(y_test, presumptions) review = recall_score(y_test, presumptions) f1 = f1_score(accuracy}')
print(f'Precision: { precision}')
print(f'Recall: { recall}')

print(f'F1 Score: { f1') 4.6.2 Lose the Faith Evaluations Python Copy code from sklearn.metrics import mean_squared_error, r2_score # It is possible to anticipate figures mse = mean_squared_error(y_test, assumptions) r2 = r2_score(y_test, figures) print(f'Mean Settled Blend: mse}')
print(f'R-squared: { r2}')

4.7 Cross-Backing

Cross-support is a system used to frame how well a model summarizes to a free dataset. It includes figuring out the data into various cross-over and making the model and mulling over everything rather than various blends.

4.7.1 Cross-Endorsement in Python: Copying code from sklearn.model_selection and importing cross_val_score #

Assuming you have a classifier model cross_val_scores = cross_val_score(model, X, y, cv=5) # Five-wrinkle cross-endorsement print(f' cross_val_scores}')
print(f'Mean Cross-Backing Score: { cross_val_scores = cross_val_score(model, X, y, cv=5, scoring='neg_mean_squared_error')
print(f'Cross-Support Scores:'')
4.7.2 Cross-Endorsement for Backslide Python Copy code from sklearn.model_selection import cross_val_score # Expecting a backslide model cross_val_scores')
print(f'Mean Cross-Support Score:')
cross_val_scores.mean()}')
This part gives a multifaceted method for directing made getting, covering straight apostatize, chose fall away from the confidence, decision trees, and unpredictable boondocks. You will devise an

effective strategy for preparing models, creating gauges, and evaluating their performance using various assessments. The going with segments will bounce into extra made subjects and genuine motivations behind mechanized thinking.

Part 5: Prologue to Solo Learning

Solo learning is the most common way of working with unlabeled information to track down associations, examples, or models in the information. This part presents the significant considerations of independent learning and its applications.

5.2 K-Means Clumping K-Means

Bunching is a conspicuous free learning system that portions information into certain parties thinking about resemblances.

5.2.1 Completing K-Means Get-together

python
Copy code
from sklearn.cluster import KMeans

```python
# Getting through 'X' is your part grid
kmeans = KMeans(n_clusters=3) # Set how much friendly events
kmeans.fit(X)

# Appropriate social affairs to each basic snippet of data
names = kmeans.labels_

# Envision the get-togethers
plt.xlabel('Feature 1')
plt.ylabel('Feature 2')
plt.title('K-Means Get-together')
plt.show()
```

5.3 Different evened out Social affair

Different evened out party makes a tree-like plan of packs, uncovering connection between pieces of data.

5.3.1 Executing Different evened out Gathering

python
Copy code

```python
# Process the linkage affiliation
linkage_matrix = linkage(X, method='ward')

# Plot the dendrogram
dendrogram(linkage_matrix)
plt.xlabel('Data Center interests')
plt.ylabel('Distance')
plt.title('Hierarchical Gathering Dendrogram')
plt.show()
```

5.4 Head Part Appraisal (PCA)

PCA is a dimensionality decline procedure that changes high-layered data into a lower-layered depiction while saving the significant information.

5.4.1 Completing Head Part Evaluation

```
python
Copy code

# Getting through 'X' is your part framework
pca = PCA(n_components=2) # Set how much parts
X_pca = pca.fit_transform(X)

# Picture the diminished layered data

plt.xlabel('Principal Fragment 1')
plt.ylabel('Principal Fragment 2')
plt.title('PCA Sharpness')
plt.show()
```

5.5 Model Assessment With the expectation of complimentary Learning

Assessing free learning models can challenge since there are no express names. Nevertheless, estimations like the blueprint score and the

Davies-Bouldin record can give information into the level of bundling.

5.5.1 Framework Score

python
Copy code

```python
from sklearn.metrics import silhouette_score

# Expecting 'X' and 'names' are open
silhouette_avg = silhouette_score(X, marks)
print(f'Silhouette Score: {silhouette_avg}')
```

5.5.2 Davies-Bouldin Once-finished

python
Copy code

```python
from sklearn.metrics import davies_bouldin_score
```

```
# Getting through 'X' and 'inscriptions' are open
db_index = davies_bouldin_score(X, names)
print(f'Davies-Bouldin Once-finished: { db_index)
```

This portion looks at solo learning and its applications, including head part assessment (PCA), different leveled out get-together, and K-Means packaging. You'll get involved experience doing these techniques and investigating free learning models using fitting appraisals. The going with parts will examine likewise made subjects in man-made cognizance and guide you through authentic applications.

Segment 6: Preamble to Mind Associations

6.1 Basics of Mind Associations

Cerebrum networks are computational models spurred by

the human brain's development and capacity. This fragment presents the focal thoughts of cerebrum associations, including neurons, layers, sanctioning capacities, and the feedforward connection.

6.1.1 Neurons and Layers A brain network is comprised of hubs, or neurons, that are associated with each other.

Neurons are facilitated into layers: an information layer, three layers that are covered up, and a result layer.

Information streams from the data layer through the mystery layers to the outcome layer.

6.1.2 Activation Functions Activation functions, which introduce non-linearity into the system, enable the network to learn complex patterns.

The sigmoid, tanh, and corrected straight unit (ReLU) are normal initiation capabilities.

6.2 Using TensorFlow and Keras

To Make a Basic Brain Organization TensorFlow and Keras are popular Python libraries for making brain organizations. This section walks you through the process of creating an easy brain network for a parallel characterization problem.

6.2.1 Presenting TensorFlow and Keras

hammer

Copy code

```
pip present tensorflow
```

6.2.2 Construction a Mind Association

python

Copy code

```
import tensorflow as tf
```

```python
from       tensorflow.keras      import
Progressive
from             tensorflow.keras.layers
import Thick

# Expecting 'X' is your part
organization and 'y' is the objective
variable
model = Progressive()

# Add a data layer
model.add(Dense(units=8,
input_dim=X.shape[1],
activation='relu'))

# Add a mystery layer
model.add(Dense(units=4,
activation='relu'))

# Add the outcome layer
model.add(Dense(units=1,
activation='sigmoid'))
```

```python
# Organize the model
model.compile(optimizer='adam', loss='binary_crossentropy', metrics=['accuracy'])
```

6.3 Planning and Surveying Cerebrum Associations

Setting up a cerebrum network incorporates changing its heaps to restrict the qualification among expected and certifiable outcomes. This section covers training, making predictions, and evaluating the model's performance.

6.3.1 Arrangement the Model

python
Copy code

```python
# Anticipating 'X_train', 'y_train' are your readiness data
model.fit(X_train, y_train, epochs=10, batch_size=32, validation_split=0.2)
```

6.3.2 Making Conjectures

```
python
Copy code
# Expecting 'X_test' is your test data
predictions_nn                          =
model.predict(X_test)
```

6.3.3 Evaluating the Model

```
python
Copy code
# Expecting 'y_test' is your test
marks
mishap,           precision           =
model.evaluate(X_test, y_test)
print(f'Loss: { loss and Precision:
accuracy}')
```

This part gives an essential understanding of cerebrum associations, guiding you through building a clear mind network using TensorFlow/Keras. The essentials of model engineering, preparing, forecast, and execution assessment will be covered. Coming about areas will examine advanced cerebrum network designs and applications in various spaces.

Part 7: Normal Language Managing (NLP)

7.1 Prelude to NLP

Normal Language Managing (NLP) is a field of man-made comprehension that brilliant lights on the correspondence among PCs and human vernaculars. This piece presents the center considerations of NLP and its applications, featuring the difficulties and huge entrances in understanding and managing human language.

7.1.1 Text Sorting out Using NLP: deciding the significance of unstructured text.

Making sense of the language: Deciphering text starting with one language then onto the accompanying.

Feeling Assessment: Closing the evaluation conferred in a piece of text.

Named Part Certification (NER): Perceiving parts like names, districts, and affiliations.

7.2 Text Preprocessing In NLP

the most widely recognized approach to cleaning and arranging unrefined text data for assessment is known as text preprocessing. Typical procedures for preprocessing text are analyzed in this part.

7.2.1 Tokenization To tokenize a text, individual words or tokens are isolated.

python
Duplicate code

```
text = "Standard Language Dealing with is entrancing!"
tokens = word_tokenize(text)
print(tokens)
```

7.2.2 Shedding Stopwords

Stopwords are unmistakable words that don't convey gigantic importance and are as frequently as conceivable cleared out from the text.

7.2.3 Lemmatization reduces words to their base or root structure. Python Copy code from nltk.corpus import stopwords stop_words = set(stopwords.words('english')) filtered_tokens = [word for word in tokens if word.lower() not in stop_words] print(filtered_tokens)

python
Duplicate code

```
from          nltk.stem          import
WordNetLemmatizer

lemmatizer                            =
WordNetLemmatizer()
lemmatized_tokens                     =
[lemmatizer.lemmatize(word)     for
word in filtered_tokens]
print(lemmatized_tokens)
```

7.3 Text Social affair with NLP

Text depiction integrates giving out predefined portrayals or names to a piece of text. This piece guides you through building an immediate text gathering model utilizing NLP.

7.3.1 The Sack of-Words (BoW) Model

The Pack of-Words model treats message as an unpredictable combination of words paying little heed to word solicitation or sentence structure.

python
Duplicate code

```python
# Expecting 'X' is an outline of text records and 'y' is the relating marks


vectorizer = CountVectorizer()
X_train_bow = vectorizer.fit_transform(X_train)
X_test_bow = vectorizer.transform(X_test)

# Create and set up a Straightforward Bayes classifier
classifier = MultinomialNB()
classifier.fit(X_train_bow, y_train)

# Make suppositions
suppositions = classifier.predict(X_test_bow)

# Overview the model
```

```
precision = accuracy_score(y_test, suppositions)
report = classification_report(y_test, suppositions)
print(f'Accuracy: { accuracy)
print(f'Classification Report:")
```

This section introduces the field of natural language processing (NLP), outlining its main ideas and applications. It guides you through text preprocessing systems like tokenization, abstaining from stopwords, and lemmatization. Likewise, it shows how to utilize the Bunch of Words (BoW) model to make a text request model. Following fragments will plunge into extra made NLP subjects and applications.

Part 8: Support Learning (Discretionary)

8.1 Prologue to Support Learning

Support Learning (RL) is a sort of AI where a specialist figures out how to pursue choices by connecting with a climate. The specialist gets criticism as remunerations or disciplines in view of its activities, permitting it to become familiar with the ideal conduct through experimentation.

8.1.1 Key Ideas

Specialist: the entity that makes choices and takes actions.

Environment: The outside framework with which the specialist interfaces.

State: The ongoing circumstance or design of the climate.

Action: The choice or move made by the specialist.

Reward: The criticism from the climate demonstrating the allure of the specialist's activity.

Policy: The system or planning from states to activities that the specialist follows.

8.2 Q-Learning

Q-Learning is a sans model support learning calculation that learns a strategy, addressed by the Q-capability, to streamline the combined compensation after some time.

8.2.1 Implementation of the Q-Table python Copy code import numpy as np # Define the environment states = [0, 1, 2, 3] # Example states actions = [0, 1] # Initialize the Q-table Q = np.zeros((len(states), len(actions))) # Q-learning parameters alpha = 0.1 # Learning rate gamma = 0.9 # Discount factor

```
# Q-learning algorithm for episode
in range(num
    state = initial_state
    while not terminal_state:
        activity = select_action(state)
        next_state,        reward        =
take_action(state, activity)
        Q[state, action] = (1 - alpha) *
Q[state, action] + alpha * (reward +
gamma * np.max(Q[next_state, :]))
        state = next_state
```

8.3 Profound Q Organizations (DQN)

Profound Q Organizations (DQN) stretch out Q-Figuring out how to deal with high-layered state spaces utilizing profound brain organizations.

8.3.1 DQN Execution with TensorFlow/Keras

python

Duplicate code

```python
import tensorflow as tf
from tensorflow.keras import Consecutive
from tensorflow.keras.layers import Thick
from tensorflow.keras.optimizers import Adam

# Fabricate the DQN model
model = Sequential([
    Dense(64, activation='relu', input_shape=(state_space,)),
    Dense(64, activation='relu'),
    Dense(action_space, activation='linear')    # Straight enactment for Q-values
])

model.compile(optimizer=Adam(learning_rate=0.001), loss='mse')   # Mean Squared Mistake misfortune

# DQN preparing circle
```

```python
for episode in range(num_episodes):
    state = initial_state
    while not terminal_state:
        # Select activity utilizing epsilon-covetous system
        activity = epsilon_greedy_action(state)

        # Make a move, see next state and prize
        next_state, reward = take_action(state, activity)

        # Update the Q-esteem utilizing the Bellman condition
        target = reward + gamma * np.max(model.predict(next_state.reshape(1, - 1)))
        q_values = model.predict(state.reshape(1, - 1))
        q_values[0][action] = target
```

```
# Train the model
model.fit(state.reshape(1, - 1), q_values, epochs=1, verbose=0)

state = next_state
```

This discretionary part gives a prologue to Support Learning (RL) and covers Q-Learning, a basic RL calculation. Furthermore, it presents Profound Q Organizations (DQN) as a strong expansion that can deal with complex state spaces. Execution subtleties utilizing a Q-table and an essential DQN model with TensorFlow/Keras are incorporated. Ensuing parts can investigate further developed RL calculations and genuine applications.

Section 9: Sending AI Models (Discretionary)

9.1 Sending out Models

Whenever you're prepared and assessed your AI model, the following stage is to convey it for use underway. This segment covers how to commodity and save your prepared model for future sending.

9.1.1 Sending out a Scikit-Learn Model

```python
Duplicate code
import joblib


# Accepting 'model' is your prepared Scikit-Learn model
joblib.dump(model, 'trained_model.joblib')
```

9.1.2 Sending out a TensorFlow/Keras Model

```python
```

Duplicate code

```
# Accepting 'model' is your prepared TensorFlow/Keras model
model.save('trained_model.h5')
```

9.2 Structure a Straightforward Web Application for Model Sending

Sending an AI model frequently includes making an easy to use interface for clients to cooperate with. This part exhibits constructing a basic web application involving Flagon for model organization.

9.2.1 Introducing Flagon

slam

Duplicate code

```
pip introduce flagon
```

9.2.2 Making a Straightforward Jar Application

python

Duplicate code

```python
from flagon import Jar, render_template, demand
import joblib
import numpy as np

application = Flask(__name__)

# Load the prepared model
model = joblib.load('trained_model.joblib')

@app.route('/')
def home():
    return render_template('index.html')

@app.route('/foresee', methods=['POST'])
def foresee():
    if request.method == 'POST':
        features = [float(x) for x in request.form.values()] # Assuming input features come from a form,
```

```python
    prediction = model.predict(input_data)
    return render_template('index.html', prediction=f' The predicted value is: prediction[0]}')

if __name__ == '__main__':
    app.run(debug=True)
```

9.2.3 HTML Layout (index.html)

html

Duplicate code

```html
<! DOCTYPE html>
<html lang="en">
<head>
    <meta charset="UTF-8">
    <meta name="viewport" content="width=device-width, starting scale=1.0">
    <title>Machine Learning Model Deployment</title>
</head>
<body>
```

<h1>Machine Learning Model Deployment</h1>
<structure method="post" action="/predict">
<!-- Input fields for highlights -->
<mark for="feature1">Feature 1:</label>
<input type="text" name="feature1" required>

<mark for="feature2">Feature 2:</label>
<input type="text" name="feature2" required>

<!-- Whenever necessary, add additional input fields: -> Predict (button type="submit">Predict) (form>) % if prediction % (h2>) % endif % (/body>) /html> This optional chapter focuses on the deployment aspect of machine

learning models. It shows how to send out a prepared model and construct a straightforward web application involving Carafe for organization. The web application permits clients to enter highlights, and the model predicts and shows the result. In more advanced chapters, additional deployment considerations, such as scaling for production, can be investigated.

Part 10: Best Practices and Future Headings

10.1 Model Interpretability

Model interpretability is essential for understanding and believing AI models, particularly in touchy areas. Model interpretability best practices are discussed in this section.

10.1.1 Feature Importance To comprehend how each feature affects model predictions, employ methods like permutation importance or SHAP values.
python
Duplicate code
# Model utilizing change significance with scikit-learn
from sklearn.inspection import permutation_importance

```
# Expecting 'model' is your prepared model and 'X_test' is your test information
result = permutation_importance(model, X_test, y_test, n_repeats=10, random_state=42)
significance = result.importances_mean
```

10.1.2 LIME (Neighborhood Interpretable Model-skeptic Clarifications)

LIME gives locally reliable clarifications to individual expectations by annoying info highlights.

```
python Import lime_tabular
explainer = lime_tabular and use LIME with scikit-learn from lime as an example.
LimeTabularExplainer(X_train, feature_names=X_train.columns, class_names=['class_0', 'class_1'])
```

```
clarification                          =
explainer.explain_instance(X_test.il
oc[0],          model.predict_proba,
num_features=len(X_train.columns)
)
```

10.2 Morals in AI

Moral contemplations in AI are significant to guarantee fair and unprejudiced models. Best practices and guidelines for ethical machine learning are discussed in this section.

10.2.1 Reasonableness and Inclination

Consistently evaluate and moderate predispositions in preparing information and model expectations to guarantee fair results.

10.2.2 Straightforwardness

Obviously impart the objectives and limits of your models, and give clarifications to show expectations.

10.2.3 Security

Defend client information and guarantee consistence with information insurance guidelines.

10.3 Future Patterns in AI

AI is a quickly developing field. This segment investigates arising patterns and future headings.

10.3.1 Reasonable simulated intelligence (XAI)

Proceeded with accentuation on making AI models more interpretable and reasonable.

10.3.2 Unified Learning

Preparing AI models across decentralized gadgets while saving security.

10.3.3 AutoML (Mechanized AI)

Mechanization of the start to finish interaction of applying AI to certifiable issues.

10.3.4 Support Learning Headways

Further headways in support learning, particularly in complex spaces.

10.3.5 Quantum AI

Investigation of the convergence between quantum registering and AI.

This section centers around best practices and future headings in AI. It covers model interpretability, moral contemplations, and arising patterns like logical simulated intelligence, combined learning, AutoML, and progressions in support learning and quantum AI. Remaining informed about these patterns will be fundamental for experts and analysts in the field.

End

Congrats on finishing this exhaustive manual for AI with Python for fledglings! You've set out on a journey that covered fundamental ideas, how to put them into practice, and optional explorations of more complex topics. Let's go over the main points:

Prologue to AI: Learn about the fundamentals, types, and applications of machine learning in various fields.

Setting Up Your Current circumstance: Figure out how to set up an AI climate utilizing Python, Boa constrictor, and fundamental libraries.

Exploratory Information Investigation (EDA): Investigate methods for stacking, cleaning, and picturing information, establishing the groundwork for compelling AI.

Supervised Instruction: Plunge into the universe of administered learning with direct relapse, strategic relapse, choice trees, irregular woodlands, and model assessment procedures.

Unaided Learning: Investigate solo learning strategies, including K-Means bunching, progressive grouping, and head part examination (PCA).

Prologue to Brain Organizations: Dive into the essentials of brain organizations, construct a basic model utilizing TensorFlow/Keras, and figure out how to prepare and assess brain organizations.

Processing of natural language (NLP): Find the essentials of NLP, including message preprocessing and message characterization utilizing the Sack of-Words model.

Support Learning (Discretionary): Alternatively investigate support learning ideas, including Q-Learning and Profound Q Organizations.

Sending AI Models (Discretionary): Learn how to use Flask to create a straightforward web app for model deployment and export trained models.

Best Practices and Directions for the Future: Investigate best practices in model interpretability, morals in AI, and future patterns like logical artificial intelligence, united learning, AutoML, and quantum AI.

As you proceed with your process in AI, recall that it's a powerful field with consistent headways. Remain inquisitive, investigate new themes, and apply your insight to certifiable issues. The abilities you've developed will provide a solid foundation for any endeavor, be it application development, research, or challenging problem-solving.

Continue to learn, remain drew in with the local area, and embrace the astonishing difficulties and open doors that AI offers. Best of luck on your AI process!